Y0-AEX-117

LET'S GO

Workbook

1

by
S. Wilkinson
R. Nakata
K. Frazier

Oxford University Press

Unit 1

Trace and connect.

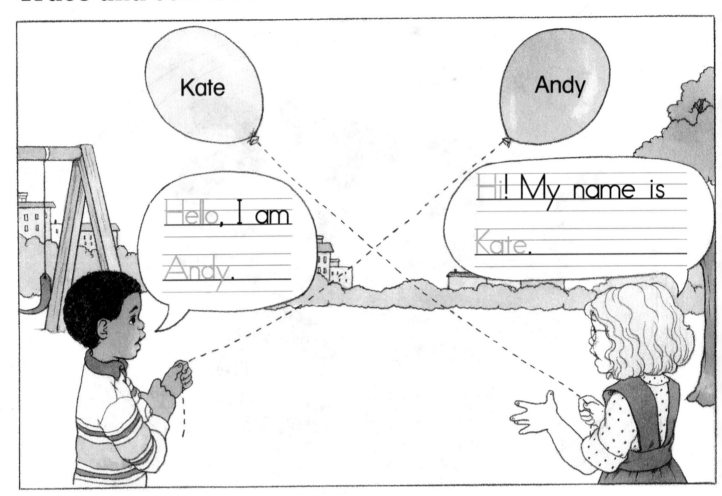

Write your name.

My name is _____.

Trace.

What is this?

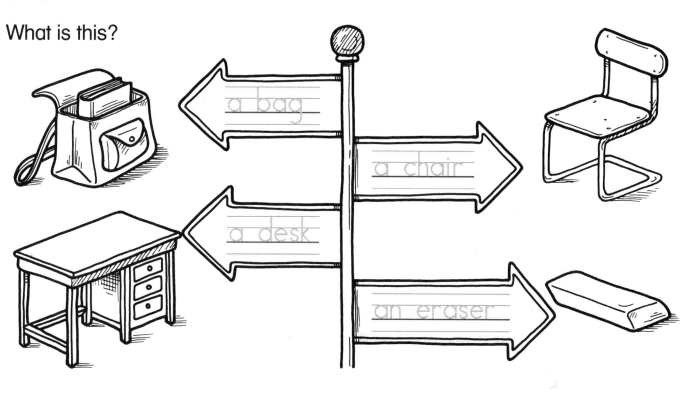

a bag

a chair

a desk

an eraser

Trace.

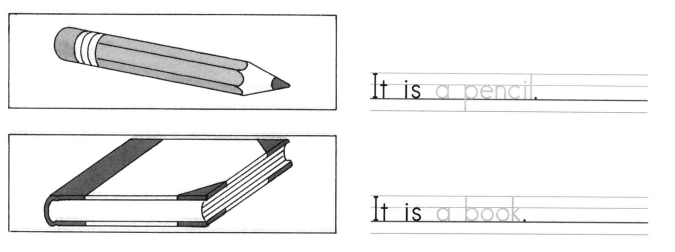

It is a pencil.

It is a book.

Draw and write.

It is _____.

2

Circle the answer.

Is this a pencil?

Yes, it is.

No, it is not.

Is this a book?

Yes, it is.

No, it is not.

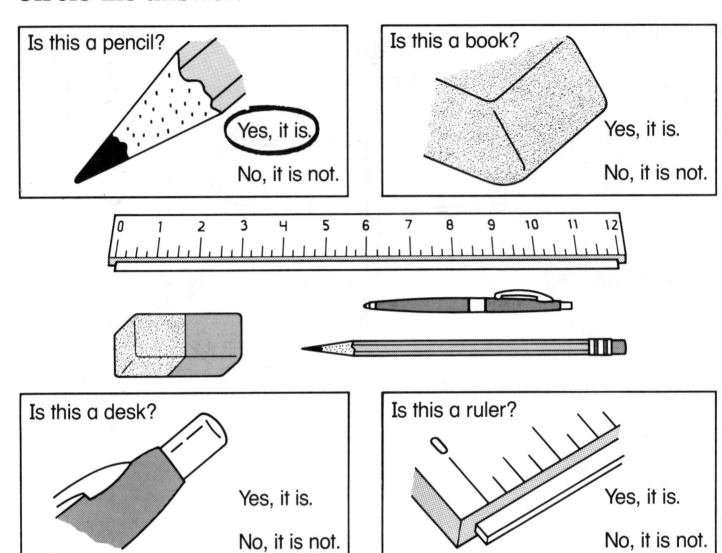

Is this a desk?

Yes, it is.

No, it is not.

Is this a ruler?

Yes, it is.

No, it is not.

Trace.

Is this a desk?

Yes, it is.

Is this a chair?

No, it is not.

Trace. Connect the letters.

A a b c d e f g h i j k l m n

B
C
D
E
F
G
H
I
J
K
L
M

o
p
q
r
s
t
u
v
w
x
y
z

N O P Q R S T U V W X Y Z

4

Trace.

Please be quiet.

Point to the teacher.

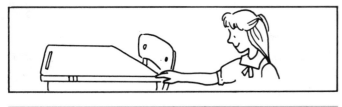

Touch your desk.

Listen carefully.

Match and trace.

Open your book.

Close your book.

Stand up.

Sit down.

Circle and trace.

What is this?

a book

a bag

It is a book.

What is this?

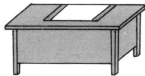

a chair

a desk

It is a desk.

Circle and write.

What is this?

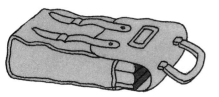

a bag

a pencil

It is _____ .

Trace.

Is this a ruler?

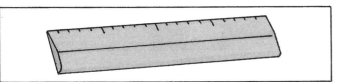

Yes, it is.

Is this a pen?

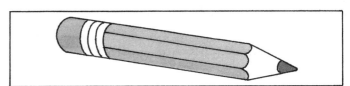

No, it is not.

Write.

Is this an eraser?

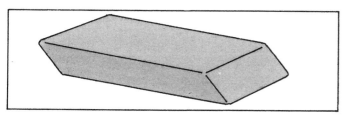

_____ , it is.

Unit 2

Trace.

Trace.

7

Trace, color, and write.

red

yellow

black

green

orange

brown

purple

pink

blue

gray

What color is this?

It is _____ .

8

Color and trace.

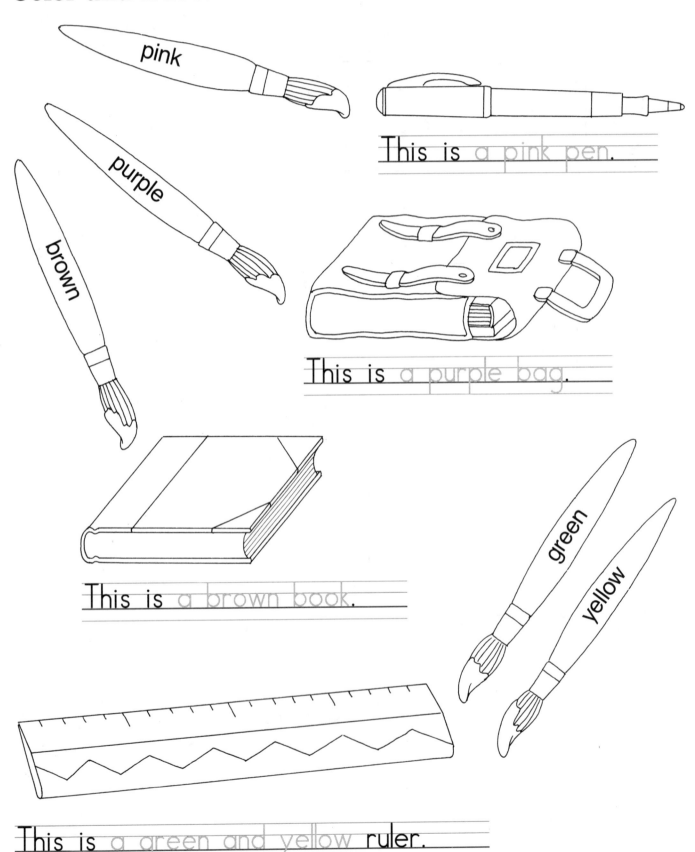

pink

purple

brown

This is a pink pen.

This is a purple bag.

This is a brown book.

green

yellow

This is a green and yellow ruler.

Connect and trace.

A a   B b   C c

book   cat   apple

Circle.

a   b   c   a   b   c   a   b   c

Trace.

a   apple   A   Andy

b   book   b   bag

C   cat   c   cloud

Connect and say.

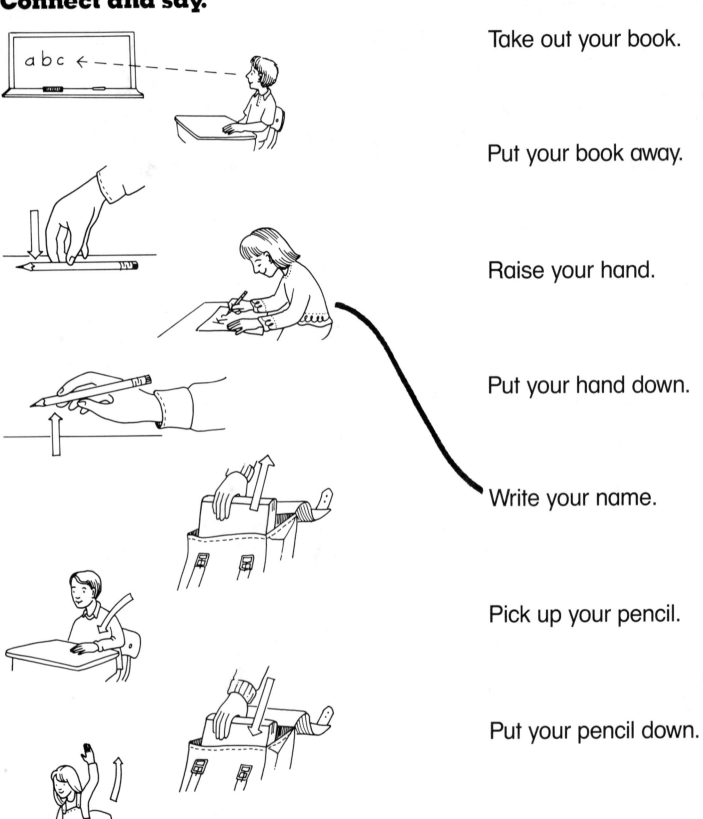

Take out your book.

Put your book away.

Raise your hand.

Put your hand down.

Write your name.

Pick up your pencil.

Put your pencil down.

Look at the board.

11

Color, trace, and write.

red   yellow   blue   green

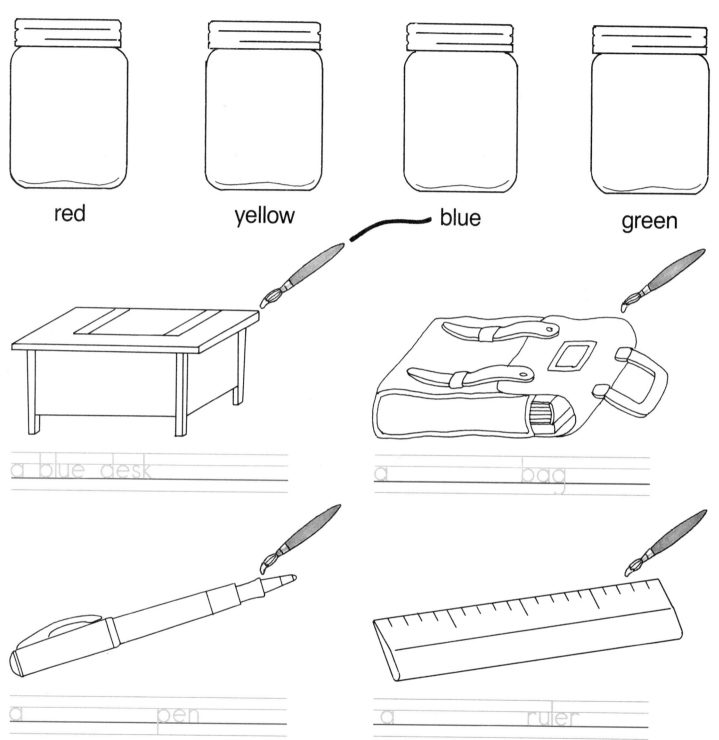

a blue desk   a _____ bag

a _____ pen   a _____ ruler

Trace the alphabet.

a b c d e f g h i j k l m n o p q r s t u v w x y z

Review

1. Trace.

m	A	q	E	F	G	e	L	a	b
P	B	C	D	Q	H	k	y	D	c
r	S	o	W	f	I	M	p	e	d
T	u	M	L	K	J	c	J	f	R
P	O	N	g	Y	j	i	h	g	N
Q	w	n	I	l	k	G	i	Q	e
R	S	T	U	m	n	s	t	u	v
o	H	f	V	F	o	r	X	S	w
t	Y	X	W	I	p	q	J	y	x
B	Z	j	k	K	v	E	r	z	N

2. Connect and write.

A a

B b

C c

___at

_apple

___ook

3. Circle and write.

What is this?

a book

a bag

It is _____.

What is this?

a pen

a ruler

It is _____.

4. Write and color.

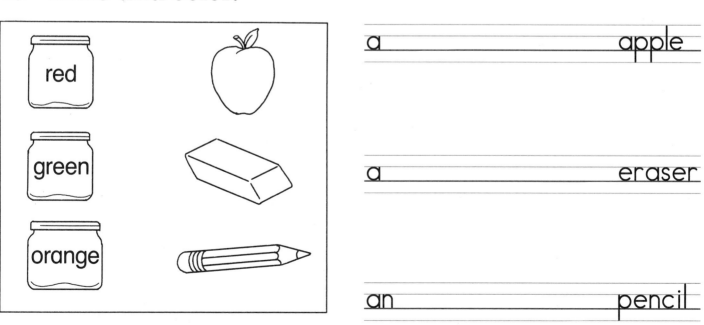

red

green

orange

a _____ apple

a _____ eraser

an _____ pencil

Unit 3

Connect and trace.

Trace, write, and draw.

This is my friend,   .

Circle.

a table
(tables)

a pen

pens

a notebook

notebooks

a pencil case

pencil cases

a marker

markers

a desk

desks

Circle and trace.

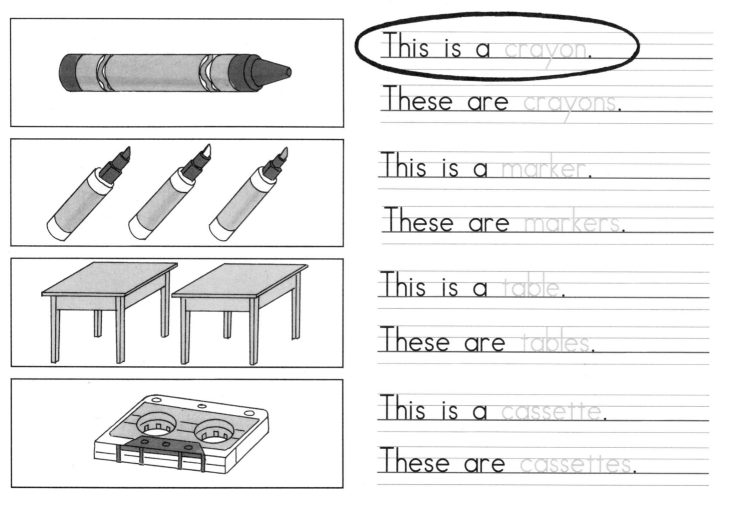

This is a crayon.

These are crayons.

This is a marker.

These are markers.

This is a table.

These are tables.

This is a cassette.

These are cassettes.

Trace, match, and write.

five

seven

ten

eight

two

three

nine

six

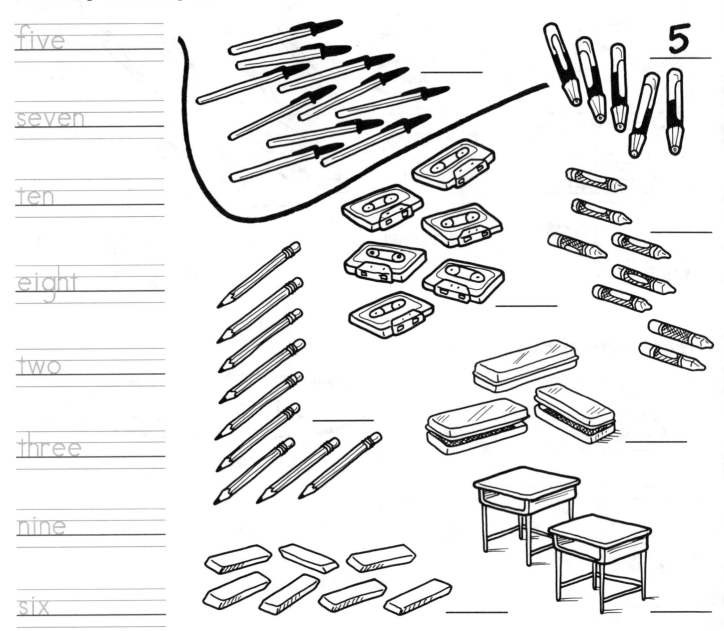

5

Trace.

one cat

four crayons

17

Connect and trace.

fish

desk

egg

Trace.

d desk dog door d

e egg eraser eight e

f fish four five f

Match and say.

Go to the door.

Make a circle.

Make two lines.

Give me the crayon.

Draw a picture.

Come here.

Circle, write, and trace.

Count the boys.

one

two

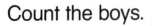

Count the girls.

four

five

girls

Circle.

this
these

this
these

this
these

Circle and write.

This
These

This
These

_____ is a marker.

_____ are pens.

Circle, write, and trace.

How many?

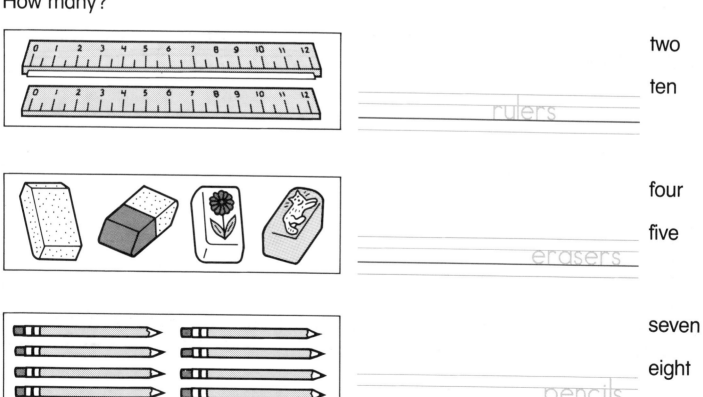

two
ten

_____ rulers

four
five

_____ erasers

seven
eight

_____ pencils

Unit 4

Trace.

It's nice to meet you.

It's nice to meet you, too.

Draw and trace.

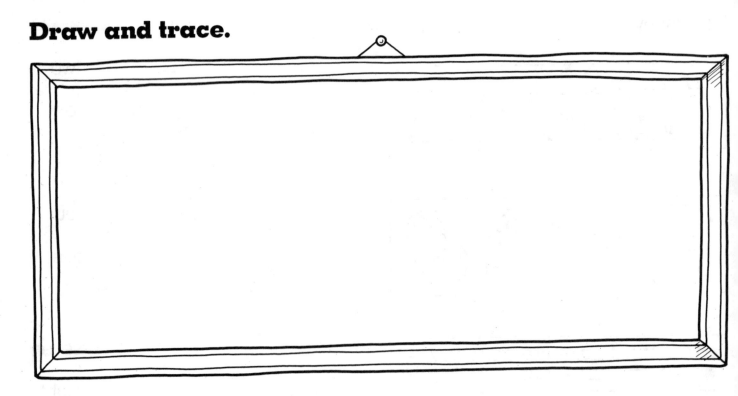

This is my family.

Trace.

Who is he?

He is my father.

He is my brother.

Who is she?

She is my sister.

She is my grandmother.

Circle.

he

she

he

she

he

she

22

Connect and trace.

old

fat

ugly

pretty

young

thin

Circle, trace, and write.

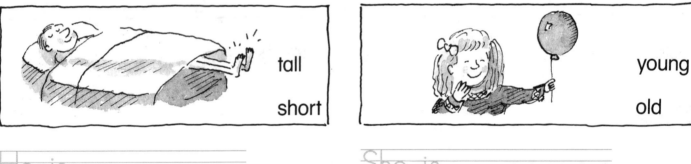

tall

short

young

old

He is _____ .

She is _____ .

ugly

pretty

fat

thin

She is _____ .

He is _____ .

Trace.

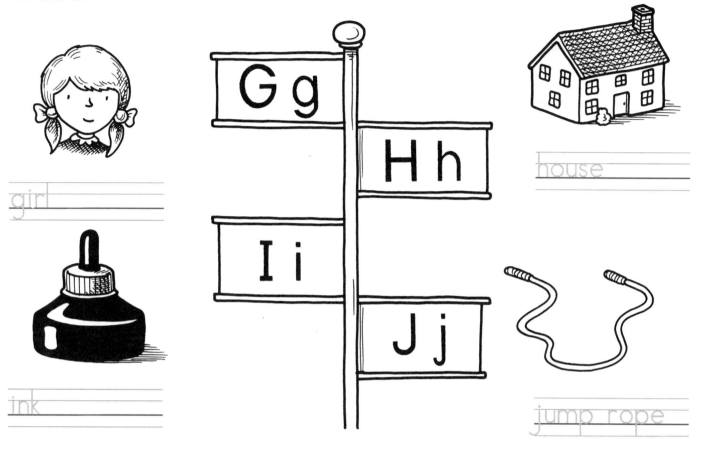

girl

ink

house

jump rope

Circle and write.

g
(h)
i
j

house

g
h
i
j

__nk

G
H
I
J

__enny

g
h
i
j

__randfather

Match and trace.

go to sleep

wake up

eat dinner

clean up

play the piano

do your homework

Trace.

Don't watch TV.

Don't make a mess.

25

Circle and trace.

He is ugly.

He is pretty.

She is old.

She is young.

She is tall.

She is short.

Connect and trace.

sister

grandfather

mother

brother

grandmother

father

Review

1. Write.

Across   Down

3.

1.

5.

2.

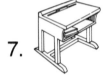
7.

4.

6.

2. Circle.

he

she

he

she

he

she

he

she

3. Trace and connect.

one

eight   three

two   four

five

six

seven

| 1 | 2 | 3 | 4 | 5 | 6 | 7 | 8 |

4. Write.

old
young

tall
short

He is _____ .

She is _____ .

She is _____ .

He is _____ .

Unit 5

Count and write.

I am 6 years old.

I am ___ years old.

I am ___ years old.

Trace, write, and draw.

How old are you?

I am ___ years old.

Trace.

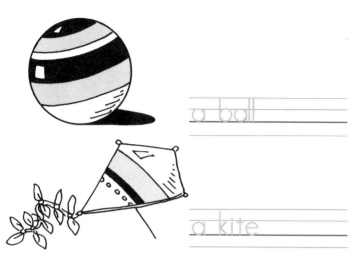

a ball

a kite

a car

a doll

Trace and write.

What is it?

It is _____.

What is it?

It is _____.

What is it?

It is _____.

What is it?

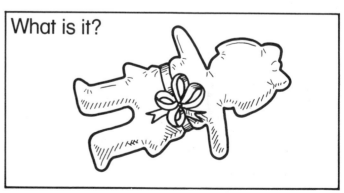

It is _____.

30

Circle and trace.

Is it a yo-yo?

Yes, it is.

No, it is not.

Yes, it is.

Is it a jump rope?

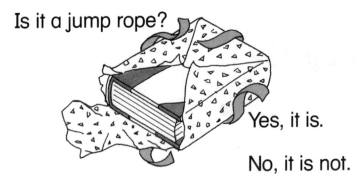

Yes, it is.

No, it is not.

No, it is not.

Circle and write.

Is it a bicycle?

Yes, it is.

No, it is not.

Is it a robot?

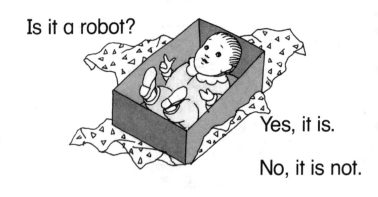

Yes, it is.

No, it is not.

Circle and write.

big

little

big

little

a   cat

a   cat

Trace and match.

K k   L l   M m   N n

mother   kite   notebook   lion

Circle and write.

K
L
M
N

__ate

k
l
m
n

__isten

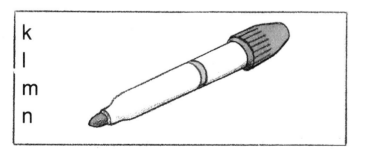

k
l
m
n

__arker

k
l
m
n

__ine

32

Match and trace.

play with a yo-yo

throw a ball

jump rope

hit a ball

Trace.

Can you do a puzzle?

Yes, I can.

Can you catch a ball?

No, I cannot.

Write.

Can you hit a ball?

Connect, trace, and write.

Is it a puzzle?

Yes, it is.

Is it a bicycle?

No, it is not.

Is it a car?

_____

_____

Is it a bat?

_____

_____

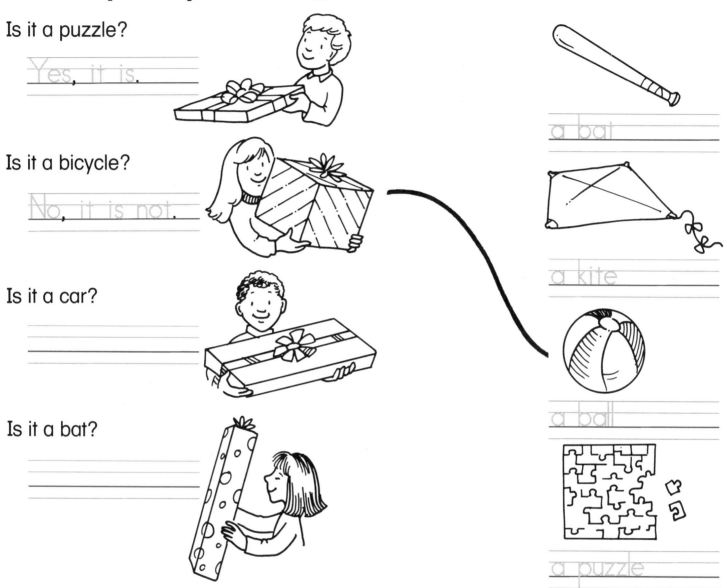

a bat

a kite

a ball

a puzzle

Circle and write.

What is it?

It is _____.

a big robot

a little robot

34

Unit 6

Trace.

How is the weather today?

It is sunny.

Match and trace.

sunny

windy

cloudy

snowy

rainy

Write and draw.

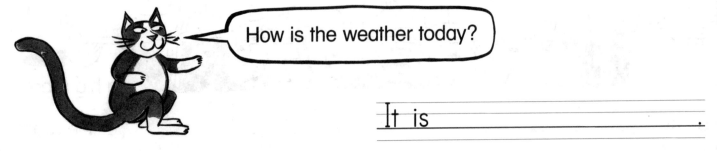

How is the weather today?

It is _____.

Circle.

|  | a flower |
| | flowers |

|  | a cloud |
| | clouds |

| 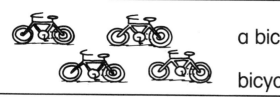 | a bicycle |
| | bicycles |

|  | a table |
| | tables |

Circle and write.

How many puddles are there?

six puddles

seven puddles

There are _____.

How many trees are there?

four trees

five trees

There are _____.

How many clouds are there?

one cloud

two clouds

There are _____.

Circle and trace.

in

on

in

on

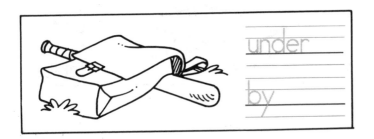

under

by

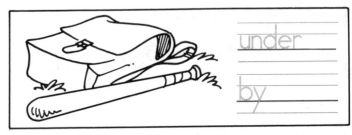

under

by

Circle and write.

Where is the book?

in

on

_____ the bag _____

Where is the bicycle?

under

by

_____ the tree _____

Where are the bats?

on

under

_____ the table _____

Where are the balls?

by

in

_____ the puddle _____

Write.

O o   __ctopus   __pen   o

P p   __en   __encil   p

Q q   __uiet   __uestion   q

R r   __uler   __ed   r

Circle and trace.

o p q r 	o p q r 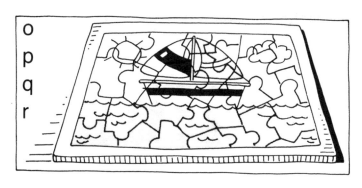
old	puzzle
o p q r 	o p q r 
question	robot

Trace and circle.

Can he play baseball?

Yes, he can.

No, he cannot.

Can she climb a tree?

Yes, she can.

No, she cannot.

Can he ride a bicycle?

Yes, he can.

No, he cannot.

Can she play tag?

Yes, she can.

No, she cannot.

Can he read a book?

Yes, he can.

No, he cannot.

Can she fly a kite?

Yes, she can.

No, she cannot.

Circle and say.

It is cloudy.

It is sunny.

It is rainy.

It is snowy.

Trace and draw.

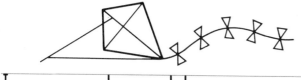

It is on the table.

It is under the table.

It is by the table.

Trace and write.

How many kites are there?

How many trees are there?

There are _____ kites.

There is _____ tree.

Review

1. Write and trace.

k l m n o p q r

___ite ___ion ___ouse

___uter ___otebook

___uestion ___encil ___ctopus

2. Find the words.

kite   bicycle   yo-yo   box

k	j	f	s	u	b	o	x	b	d	l	k	i	t	e
m	c	a	r	o	n	p	e	b	a	l	l	f	r	v
c	w	q	m	y	o	y	o	t	r	d	o	l	l	g
b	i	c	y	c	l	e	h	n	b	a	t	t	z	i

doll   ball   car   ba___

41

3. Match and trace.

big

long

round

little

short

square

4. Connect and trace.

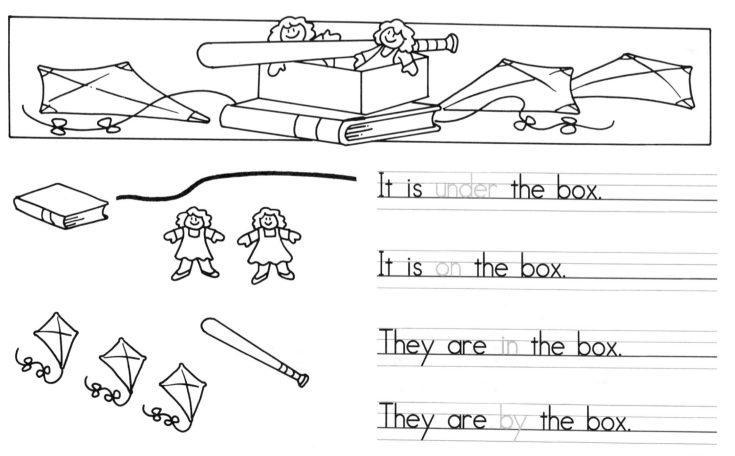

It is under the box.

It is on the box.

They are in the box.

They are by the box.

Unit 7

Trace.

an apple

juice

Trace and write.

I'm hungry. I want _____.

I'm thirsty. I want _____.

Trace.

Here you are.

Thank you.

You're welcome.

43

Trace.

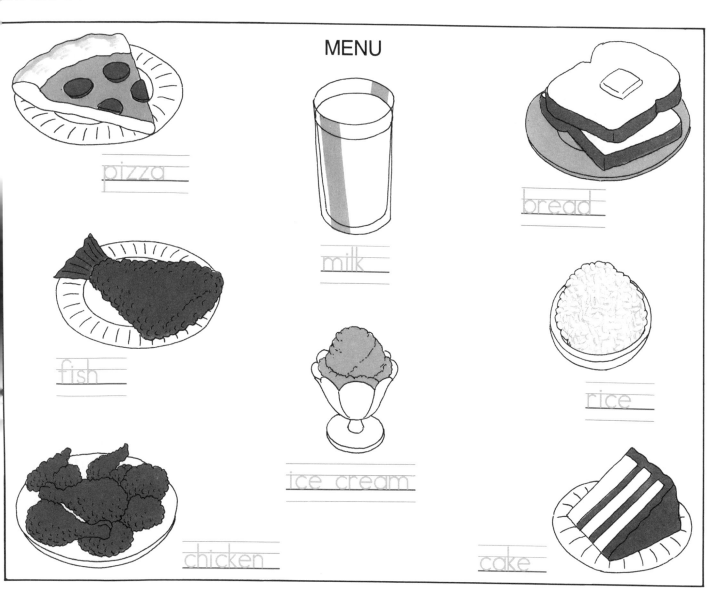

MENU

pizza

milk

bread

fish

rice

ice cream

chicken

cake

Write and draw.

What do you want?

I want _____ and _____.

Trace.

Do you want ice cream?

No, I do not.

Do you want pizza?

Yes, I do.

Circle and write.

Do you want rice?

Yes, I do.

No, I do not.

Do you want fish?

Yes, I do.

No, I do not.

Do you want cake?

Yes, I do.

No, I do not.

Do you want bread?

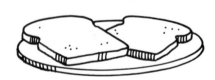

Yes, I do.

No, I do not.

Match and trace.

S s

T t

U u

V v

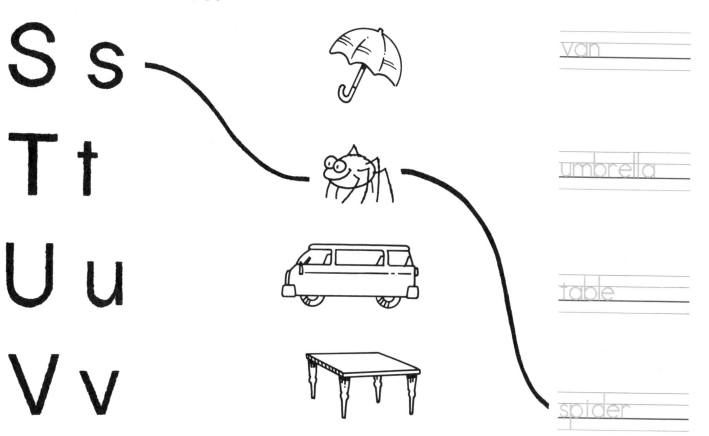

van

umbrella

table

spider

Circle and trace.

s
t
u
v

s
t
u
v

ugly

violin

s
t
u
v

s
t
u
v

sunny

tree

Trace.

buy milk

open it

pour it

drink it

buy an apple

wash it

cut it

eat it

Circle and write.

drink it

eat it

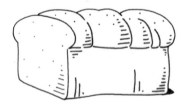

pour it

cut it

wash it

open it

pour it

wash it

47

Write.

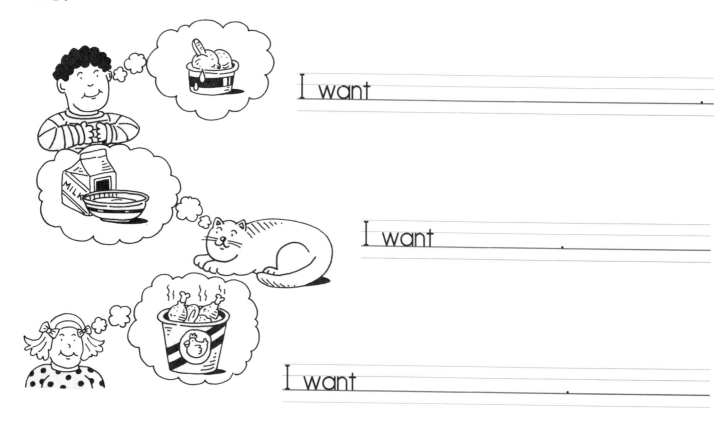

I want _____ .

I want _____ .

I want _____ .

Circle and write.

Do you want ice cream and fish?

_____

_____

Yes, I do.

No, I do not.

Do you want ice cream and cake?

_____

_____

Yes, I do.

No, I do not.

Unit 8

Color, trace, and write.

What's your favorite color?

I like _____ .

I like _____ .

I like _____ .

I like _____ .

red

blue

green

Color and write.

What about you?

pink

I like _____ .

49

Match and trace.

cats

dogs

rabbits

spiders

birds

frogs

Draw and write.

What do you like?

I like

Trace.

Do you like spiders?

No, I do not.

Do you like cats?

Yes, I do.

Write.

Do you like rabbits?

Do you like frogs?

Do you like dogs?

Do you like birds?

51

Trace and match.

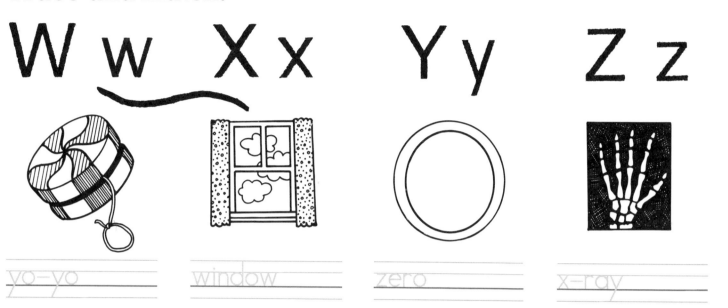

W w   X x   Y y   Z z

yo-yo   window   zero   x-ray

Trace and connect.

yellow   window   x-ray

yo-yo   zero   windy

W w   X x   Y y   Z z

Trace and match.

swim

hop

walk

run

jump

fly

Trace.

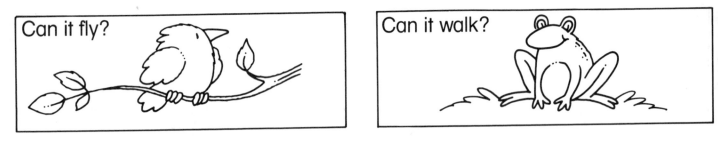

Can it fly?

Can it walk?

Yes, it can.

No, it cannot.

Write.

Can it hop?

Can it swim?

53

Write.

Look! There is _____.

Look! There is _____.

a bird

a dog

Circle, trace, and write.

What do you like?

dogs

cats

I like _____.

What do you like?

frogs

spiders

I like _____.

Circle and write.

Do you like cats?

Yes, I do.

No, I do not.

Do you like spiders?

Yes, I do.

No, I do not.

Review

1. Write.

Down

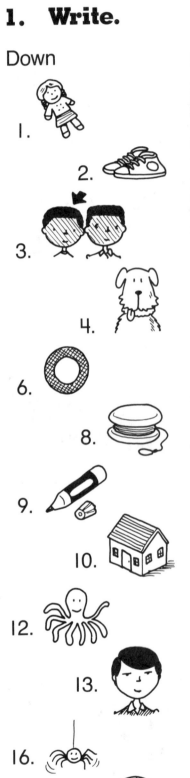

1.

2.

3.

4.

6.

8.

9.

10.

12.

13.

16.

18.

Across

3.

5.

7.

9.

11.

13.

14.

15.

17.

19.

20.

21.

2. Match, trace, and write.

dogs   cats   birds   frogs

dribs _____

grofs _____

tcsa _____

sodg   dogs _____

What do you like?

I like _____ .

3. Connect, trace, and write.

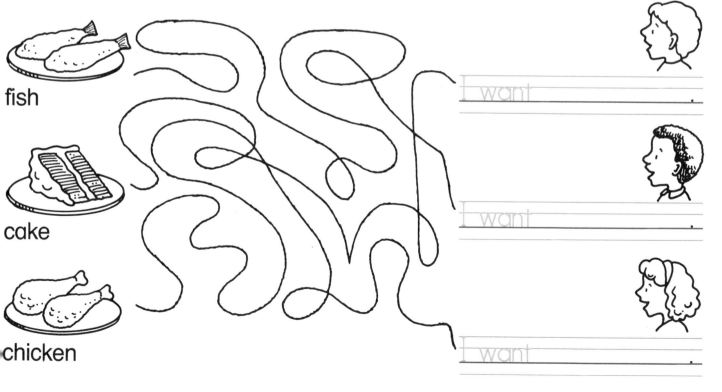

fish

cake

chicken

I want _____ .

I want _____ .

I want _____ .

Alphabet Practice

a a a

a a a

b b b

b b b

c c c

c c c

d d d

d d d

e e e

e e e

f f f

f f f

g g g

g g g

h h h

h h h

i i i

i i i

j j j

j j j

k k k

k k k

l l l

l l l

m m m

m m m

n n n

n n n

o o o

o o o

p p p

p p p

q q q

q q q

r r r

r r r

s s s

s s s

t t t

t t t

u u u

u u u

v v v

v v v

w w w

w w w

x x x

x x x

y y y

y y y

z z z

A A A

A A A

B B B

B B B

C C C

C C C

D D D

D D D

E E E

E E E

F F F

F F F

G G G

G G G

H H H

H H H

I I I

I I I

J J J

J J J

K K K

K K K

L L L

L L L

M M M

M M M

N N N

N N N

O O O

O O O

P P P

P P P

Q Q Q

Q Q Q

R R R

R R R

S S S

S S S

T T T

T T T

U U U

U U U

V V V

V V V

W W W

W W W

X X X

X X X

Y Y Y

Y Y Y

Z Z Z

Z Z Z